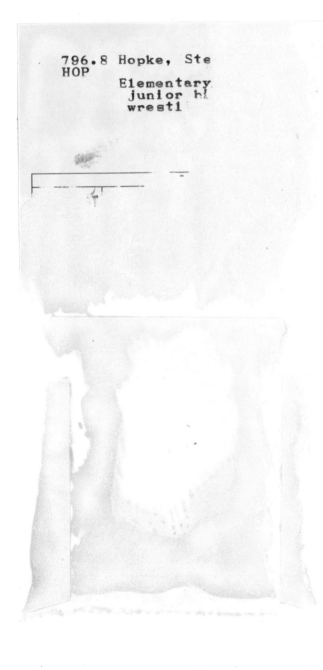

Elementary and Junior High School Wrestling

Elementary and Junior High School Wrestling

Stephen L. Hopke and Worden Kidder

South Brunswick and New York; A. S. Barnes and Company
London; Thomas Yoseloff Ltd

A. S. Barnes and Co., Inc.
Cranbury, New Jersey 08512

Thomas Yoseloff Ltd.
Magdalen House
136-148 Tooley Street
London SE1 2TT, England

Second Printing 1979

Library of Congress Cataloging in Publication Data

Hopke, Stephen L   1943–
    Elementary and junior high school wrestling.

    Bibliography: p.
    Includes index.
    1. Wrestling.   I. Kidder, M. Worden, joint author.
II. Title.
GV1195.H77   796.8'12   75-38440
ISBN 0-498-01872-5

Printed in the United States of America

Contents

Preface

With the increased number of elementary and junior high school wrestling programs being conducted throughout the country and the controversy regarding the place of wrestling at an early age, this area becomes one of prime importance to all coaches and physical education instructors. After having worked in the elementary physical education field, coached wrestling, and completed research for this book, we found a definite value in the development of a sound wrestling program for the beginning wrestler. The following recommended wrestling program is an attempt to bring together as many different sources and ideas related to the beginning wrestler as deemed necessary in developing a sound wrestling program. It is also an attempt to develop a unit in which the participant will be less apt to suffer an injury but still have the opportunity to develop wrestling skills.

Of the large number of activities presented, it is expected that each instructor will select the ones that best fit his wrestling philosophy. Attempting to incorporate all of the activities into one program may only result in a weak wrestling program with the students not learning any one activity or skill to a sufficient degree of proficiency. The wrestling activities selected for this book were those previously validated by research as being the most fundamental and safest in wrestling. There will be coaches who feel that other moves and activities can be used and are just as safe as those selected for this book. The decision as to which specific activities are to be used is left to the good judgment of each coach.

The recommendations and guidelines are for use in aiding the coach or instructor in formulating a total wrestling program. They act as standards to follow in developing a safe, sound wrestling program. If combined with the selected wrestling activities to make a total curriculum, they would reduce the chance of injury or harmful practices that may occur in vigorous sports activities at the elementary and junior high school levels.

Acknowledgments

We would like to express gratitude to the many wrestling coaches and physical education instructors in the state of Minnesota for contributing their knowledge in the formulation of the program recommendations and guidelines.

Appreciation is extended to Rosemary Johnson for the time she spent editing the manuscript. We would like to thank Dan Kidder, Dean Kidder, and Mark Bischoff who patiently posed for the illustrations and for their photographic abilities in developing the pictures.

Special recognition must be given to our wives, Jan Hopke and Barb Kidder, for the many hours they spent rereading, typing, and editing the final copy. Their support and encouragement is greatly appreciated.

Elementary and Junior High School Wrestling

1

Elementary and Junior High School Wrestling

In the past few years there has been a rapidly increasing interest in wrestling at the elementary and junior high school levels among coaches, physical education instructors, and the general public. As this interest has grown, many schools have added wrestling to their intramural sports program or physical education classes for boys in elementary and junior high grades. There are also programs that include boys in the first, second, and third grades. In some communities, local organizations have sponsored "Kid Wrestling" programs. Some of the reasons stated for considering wrestling of value in school sports programs are: (1) boys in all stages of their physical development can participate; (2) a large number of boys can participate; (3) wrestling is a natural drive in most boys; (4) wrestling is a safe and inexpensive sport. Taking the whole child into consideration, the opportunity to wrestle can contribute to his physical, social, mental, and emotional growth.

Many schools, however, have not included wrestling in their sports program because there is some question as to the effect wrestling could have on the rapidly developing bodies of boys this age. There are many physiological patterns of growth not yet developed at the pre- and early adolescent age levels. In young boys, interrupting these stages of development by injury could cause permanent damage both physically and emotionally. Other reasons stated for not including wrestling in elementary sports programs are: (1) not enough qualified instructors; (2) lack of interest by school officials; (3) not enough space or the lack of proper equipment; (4) very little available information on elementary and junior high school wrestling. It is hoped that this guide will help the instructor to overcome some of these difficulties.

It is important to possess an understanding of growth and developmental characteristics of this age and a basic knowledge of wrestling. It is also important to observe recommendations by school authorities concerning athletics and wrestling. This program is designed with these three areas in mind.

GROWTH AND DEVELOPMENTAL CHARACTERISTICS

The body parts most directly affected by an early age wrestling program are the muscles, bones, heart, lungs, and digestive system.

Two areas of prime importance are bone and heart development. Bone development continues throughout the growing years and is not completed in most cases until the individual is in his late teens or early twenties. The instructor should keep in mind that young bones are less resistant to pressure and muscle pulls, and more susceptible to deformity upon injury.

The heart, like most organs and systems in the child's body, has not yet reached its full development. Coaches must consider functional heart disturbances among young people. In some instances these disturbances may not yet be known, but could cause difficulties. The heart of the early adolescent is still not ready to support all of the activities that a highly motivated body may demand of it. Young atheletes can easily be overstimulated in such a way as to cause difficulties that may have permanent ill effects.

There is a need to keep in mind the successive stages of development that the athlete passes through in order to understand and plan for his education wisely. The rate of development varies in different individuals. Each individual matures in his own way, yet similar growth patterns are found in all boys and girls.

RECOMMENDATIONS FOR ELEMENTARY AND JUNIOR HIGH SCHOOL ATHLETICS

Some coaches and physical education instructors do not recommend wrestling for any grade at the elementary level. They suggest that wrestling should begin in the seventh grade. In the fourth through sixth grades, however, they do recommend the use of various combative activities, such as rooster fighting and leg wrestling. These activities could be considered as an introduction to a wrestling program.

It has been recommended by many wrestling coaches that a sound gymnastics unit precede the actual wrestling program. A unit of this nature would give the participant the opportunity to develop basic tumbling skills that are closely related to many rolls and moves found in wrestling. Through gymnastics the student would develop techniques in falling and absorbing shock by relaxation while landing on the mat. These techniques are important factors where safety is imperative. The basic rolls and falls found in gymnastics can be termed natural at a young age. In most young people there is little fear of being hurt. As a person grows older, he reaches a point where he must learn a move or

14

roll. The different motor mechanisms are now controlled by past experiences and habits. This learning is closely related to motor development, which is any learning directly or indirectly related to the muscular and neuromuscular systems of the body. Through the use of gymnastics and tumbling the individual will develop a much keener motor learning ability. This natural ability will tend to stay with the individual longer, as well as provide a great deal of fun and enjoyment for him.

The American Association for Health, Physical Education, and Recreation has made the following recommendations for elementary school sports:

> Sports with varying degrees of collision risk include baseball, basketball, football, hockey, soccer, softball, and wrestling. The hazards of such competition are debatable. The risks are usually associated with the conditions under which practice and play are conducted and the quality of supervision affecting the participants.

> Unless a school or community can provide exemplary supervision—medical and education—it should not undertake a program of competitive sports, especially collision sports, at a preadolescent level. In present day athletic programs many psychological factors have developed that are directly related to high pressure practices.[1]

If these factors are ignored, the school could conceivably push the young wrestler beyond the rational goals and objectives that were intended. This means that programs should be carefully supervised and certain high pressure practices should be avoided. The following is a list of undesirable practices:

> Highly organized competition in the form of leagues or championships. Overemphasis by means of newspapers, radio, television or similar media. Stress of individuals rather than teams, such as selection of "all star" teams.

> Tournaments, frequent contests, long season, "little" bowl games or other procedures that cause pressures or that may make undue physical demands on young boys or girls.

> Games or contests played at night or at other times, outside usual school or recreation hours.

> Travel beyond the immediate neighborhood (or in the case of small rural schools, a nearby community).

1. American Association for Health, Physical Education, and Recreation, *Desirable Athletic Competition for Children of Elementary School Age (Washington D.C.: AAPHER, 1968), p. 7.*

Encouragement of partisan specators and supporters—any pressures that come from social situations that place undue value on an informal game.

"Grooming" of players for a high school or college team, proselyting or inducement of any kind to cause a good player to leave his normal group and play with another team.

Commercial promotions which, under various conditions, seek to exploit youth for selfish purposes.

Competition in which a selected few players are given a large and disproportionate share of facilities and of the time and attention of staff members, with the resultant neglect of a large number of children.[2]

It is easy for an instructor or coach to lose perspective of the age and developmental levels of elementary and junior high school students. This comes about as the instructor or coach becomes deeply involved in the sport being taught. Once the sport or activity is placed first and the athlete second, undue pressure or stress can be placed on the participant both physically and emotionally. The effect that this type of pressure or stress has on an individual will depend largely on his ability to cope with it.

Doctor John L. Reichert submits the following eleven recommendations as a means of giving pre-adolescents most of the advantages and a minimum of the disadvantages in athletic programs. These recommendations are summaries of different conferences held on the topic of elementary and junior high school athletics.

1. Competition is an inherent characteristic of growing, developing children. Properly guided, it is beneficial and not harmful to their development.

2. Children should have an opportunity to develop skills in a wide variety of individual and team activities. A sound athletic program in school should include competitive and noncompetitive sports and play activities.

3. Athletics should offer an opportunity for all of the children in the school to participate in some phase of the program. Many teams are better than a few teams. At this age, the "star" system is bad.

4. Opponents should be matched as carefully as possible as to their physical and emotional level of development, as well as to their size, age, and body build.

5. Body-contact sports, particularly tackle football, boxing, and wrestling, are dangerous at this age. Touch and flag football are safe games if properly supervised.

2. American Association for Health, Physical Education, and Recreation, *Desirable Athletic Competition for Children* (Washington D.C.: AAPHER, 1962), pp. 4-5.

6. The best possible leadership should be obtained; volunteers, however well intentioned, should work under professional supervision. Parents should have a voice in the policies and administration of the program.

7. All competitive athletic programs should be organized with the cooperation of local medical organizations. All children should have a thorough physical examination before entering the program and at specified intervals during the program.

8. Regularly scheduled interschool and intercommunity contests are not recommended for this age group; neither are state, regional or national tournaments or the bowl, charity, or exhibition type of games. Commercial exploitation in any form is unequivocally condemned.

9. Any athletic program should be so designed as to be of educational as well as recreational value.

10. Provision should be made to include in some phase of the program the child who is either physically or psychologically handicapped.

11. Qualified professional leadership should be supplied. It should be such that highly organized; highly competitive programs are avoided.[3]

We believe that there is an excessive amount of youth exploitation concerning athletics at the elementary and junior high school level. One of the main reasons is the demands the public is now placing on winning in athletics. It is not uncommon to hear of state and national play-offs in many of the youth sports programs. It is no wonder boys are tired of participating in sports programs by the time they reach high school and decide to look for new and more exciting ways of having fun. Sports and competition are good wholesome ways of having fun and letting off pent-up energy, but it is important to keep it in perspective with the physical and mental levels of the participant.

WRESTLING AS A STRENUOUS SPORT

Many experts in the field of physical education feel that wrestling is one of the most strenuous sports in our culture today. Arthur H. Steinhaus listed all the major team, dual, and individual sports and rated them from low to high on a physical fitness rating scale. The areas rated were: endurance, agility, and strength (leg, abdomen, and

3. John L. Reichert, M.D., "Competitive Athletics for Pre Teen-age Children," *Journal of the American Medical Association,* 166:14 (April 5, 1958): 1701-1707.

arm-shoulder). Wrestling was the only sport that received a high rating in all areas. [4]

Endurance is an important element in preparing for participation in wrestling. Tenseness and lack of proper conditioning hinders the beginning wrestler, just as it does when he is learning many other physical skills, resulting in early fatigue. Constant attention to relaxation is necessary in order to conserve strength and to allow sufficient circulation of blood within the muscles.

JUSTIFYING WRESTLING IN THE ELEMENTARY AND JUNIOR HIGH SCHOOL

Wrestling is a sport where individuals of all shapes and sizes can compete against others of equal weight; this is one of its chief selling points. Also, certain handicapped individuals can participate in wrestling. The ability to serve a great number at a reasonable cost aids justification. The development of coordination, muscle strength, confidence, a sense of humility, an ability to protect oneself, and a realization of the importance of sacrifice are but a few of the benefits a young person may harvest from the sport.

Thousands of programs have been organized through schools, clubs, civic organizations, churches, YMCAs, and AAU. It is safe to estimate that more than one hundred thousand elementary boys are being introduced to amateur wrestling each year. These wrestlers are learning some of the basic skills, enjoying the thrill of competition, and gaining tremendously in physical fitness.

SUMMARY

While collecting information for an elementary and junior high school wrestling program, three areas were found to be important for investigation: (1) the developmental levels; (2) the question of competitive athletics for this age; and (3) wrestling as a sport for elementary and junior high school students. Under these areas there are many others containing related information.

It would appear that a coach or teacher should possess a thorough understanding of the sport and take into account the total person. He must construct the program as an instructional unit aimed at fun, not one just to develop star wrestlers. If this can be kept in mind by all persons concerned, there would be: (1) a balanced perspective between

4. Arthur H. Steinhaus, *How to Keep Fit and Like It* (Chicago: Darnell Corp., 1957), p. 29.

participation and winning; (2) reduced chance of exploitation of the participant; (3) less chance of injury, both physical and mental; (4) the promotion of a sound physical education program; and (5) enjoyment of the sport. A qualified instructor or coach, with all these concepts in mind, would have the foundation for a sound wrestling program.

2

Program

Development and Execution

Within the framework of this chapter you will find the information needed to develop and conduct a wrestling program at the elementary and junior high school levels. It is hoped that any questions a coach or instructor might have concerning wrestling at these levels will be answered. It was our intent to formulate a general wrestling program that individual coaches might adapt to fit their coaching philosophies.

PROGRAM RECOMMENDATIONS

Preparatory Activities

In preparing for a beginning wrestling program it would be wise to conduct some type of preparatory unit. This could be done in conjunction with the regularly scheduled physical education classes or as a voluntary activity much like the wrestling program. The activities involved should not be solely of conditioning, but ones that are enjoyable yet will carry over into wrestling. One such activity would be gymnastics. Gymnastics will enable the individual to improve flexibility, strength, agility, and balance. It will also give the wrestler a wider range of education experiences. A second activity that would be beneficial to the junior high age student would be weight training. A weight training program at this level should be well supervised, with the main emphasis placed on proper technique in the use of the different weights. For further description of weight training recommendations see chapter 4.

Program Availability

The wrestling program should be available to all physically able individuals grades four and up. Caution should be taken to equalize the maturation level as well as matching weight. Handicapped persons may also be able to participate in wrestling activities, depending on the extent of their disability. Many blind boys and those with missing limbs have participated successfully in competitive wrestling. If there are any questions as to a person's physical capabilities, they should be noted during the physical examination by the doctor.

Wrestling can be taught during the physical education classes and-or an intramural sports program. Out-of-school programs can be sponsored by different community organizations (see page 26). In most of these cases, school facilities will be used. Generally, interschool competition is reserved for junior and senior high schools where equipment, facilities, and supervision are adequate.

Coaching Qualifications

Those who have responsibilities to carry out the program should have a knowledgeable background in the instruction of wrestling techniques and activities. This would also include an understanding of the developmental patterns of elementary and junior high school wrestlers. The reason for this type of background is that it is easy for a coach who has no background in wrestling to lose perspective as to the physical demands required to become a wrestler. The winning objective could become too important and overshadow the real reason for this type of program. It would also be beneficial if at least one of the coaches was a teacher in the school where the program is being conducted. This would help form a link between the school and the community. In most programs, school equipment and facilities will be used. The "Kid Wrestling Programs" sponsored by the Jaycees are in many cases supervised by community volunteers. If some type of working relationship can be formed between the school and community, a better program will result.

Physical Examinations

All participants should be required to have a physical examination before participating in any type of wrestling program. If the wrestling program is being conducted within the regular physical education class, a physical would not be needed. Any time the program is conducted as an intramural activity a physical examination should be required. This is the case in the junior and senior high and no exception should be made for the elementary school. The need for physical examinations may be considered even more important for the elementary age group because of the greater chance of undiscovered impairments and the rapid physical growth taking place at this age.

Goals

The elementary school wrestling program will not achieve high standards of wrestling proficiency. To become a good wrestler takes hours of hard practice. There isn't the time, means, or need to do this with the early adolescent. The activities should be designed as a way of having fun with the enjoyment of wrestling as one of the main outcomes. As wrestling progresses to the junior high, more emphasis can be placed on the development of skills.

The wrestling program should not be concerned mainly with the development of future varsity wrestlers. If this is even implied during the different practice periods, the program should be brought to an end. There is already too much exploitation of young people for the ambitions of coaches and sports fans. If this is permitted in the elementary school sport program system, a complete overhaul is needed.

Order of Activity Introduction

The wrestling activities should proceed in order from simple to complex, the most advanced activities still being quite simple. Typically this age has a very short attention span. If the activities are allowed to become too complex for their wrestling abilities, they will easily become frustrated. If this happens, there will be the tendency for some to quit. It should be remembered that there will be individuals participating who have never wrestled, as well as some with considerable experience. The coaches should gear the activities to the individuals with the average amount of wrestling experience. If necessary, the group could be divided into smaller groups to allow for differences in wrestling proficiency. It will be necessary to do this in a way not to embarrass the low ability students. This may be done by dividing the group according to grade levels, or number of years of previous wrestling experience.

Public Viewing

The public (parents, interested spectators, etc.) should be allowed to view the wrestling program. Parents and spectators, however, can become very involved in the sport and in some cases tend to push the young wrestler into something he is not interested in or ready to do. It should be remembered that the public is only viewing, and their presence may cause severe psychological pressures to develop. It must be kept in mind that the wrestlers are participating to have fun. At no time should they be pushed to wrestle for blood or "cream the other guy." Keeping this concept in proper perspective will allow for a more wholesome teaching-learning experience.

Publicity

The use of newspaper, radio, or television publicity should be kept to a minimum. It is easy to develop pressure that should not be a part of an elementary sports program. When this type of coverage is used, it should be of the program in general and not concerned about individual winners or team championships. Pictures taken should be of everyone who participates, not just a few. If awards are to be given, again everyone should receive one. This will give every participant the *feeling of success.* Too many times the poor wrestler is just left out and forgotten; he must be equally considered. If he were not interested, he would not have come out. One good method of giving everyone a feeling of achievement is to give a participating award to everyone competing in the program.

In both public viewing and publicity, it is very important to keep winning pressure at a minimum. The goal should be to build as broad a base of participation as possible, to stimulate interest in wrestling, and to expose as many as possible to the benefits of the program. If your tournaments are held with too much publicity and pressure, you will have told the vast majority that they are losers and their self-image could be damaged. It is best to build their confidence and skills on a firm base so that when each one thinks of wrestling, he does not view himself as a loser. Not all can be winners. In conclusion, this would mean—pressure *should not* be placed on winning throughout the elementary school wrestling program, but instead instruction, learning, and accomplishment should be the prime goals. At the junior high level more recognition can be given to the winners, but all participants still should be recognized.

Weight Reduction

Weight reduction *should not* be allowed during the elementary school wrestling program. In the junior highs weight loss due to the strenuousness of the activity should be closely watched to determine if it is reasonable for the body build of the individual, and not to exceed 5 per cent of the prewrestling weight. Even the thought of losing weight for the purpose of filling a lower weight class should be condemned. It is the responsibility of the coaches to see that this does not occur. One way to avoid this problem is to have all boys weigh in at the first practice or use the physical examination weight. Their weight at that time will be recorded and considered their weight for the entire program or they will not be allowed to wrestle. When tournament weight classes are set up, they will have no choice as to where they will wrestle. The coaches' responsibility cannot be stressed enough in the matter of weight reduction.

Nutritional Consideration [1]

Optimal nutrition is one of the basic conditions necesssary to maintain top physical performance. Contrary to common beliefs, the question of nutrition for the athlete is perfectly straightforward and involves little if any mystery. The optimum diet for athletes, like nonathletes, must supply adequate water, calories, protein, fats, carbohydrates, minerals, and vitamins in suitable proportions. By virtue of his high energy expediture, the athlete in training requires a greater caloric intake than the more sedentary person to maintain body weight.

The increased caloric requirements should be provided by increasing food intake across the board without in any way significantly altering the proportions of the diet. There are no special food sources that supply extra reserves of energy that are not supplied by other foods with the same nutrients. An adequate guide on which an athlete should base his food selection is the basic food groups, which are: (1) dairy products; (2) breads and cereals; (3) fruits and vegetables; (4) meats and poultry.

A nutritional practice that is harmful and thus must be strongly discouraged is total starvation alternated with semistarvation and dehydration. This is sometimes practiced by boxers and wrestlers in order to make a lower weight classification.

Total starvation does more than dehydrate the body. The accompanying weight loss also involves loss of protein, glycogen, minerals, enzymes, and other important cell constituents. These responses diminish body reserves for athletic demands and, in the young competitor, could affect normal growth response. This practice has been condemned by the American Medical Association, since it serves the ethics of sportsmanship no better than it does the health of the athlete.

Food faddism and ignorance are more prominent in the area of athletics than in any other sphere of nutrition. Special dietary schemes

1. Adapted from "National Dairy Council", *Dairy Council Digest vol. 26, no. 2 (March - April 1975).*

and aids have been advocated by trainers and coaches to improve performance and endurance. Although these dietary schemes may have some kind of psychological advantage for the athlete, they have neither sound physiological nor nutritional bases but, rather, they are based mainly on older traditions and superstitions.

Weight, Size, and Grade Level

Wrestling should be done with boys of similar weight, size, and grade level. There will be boys who are at each extreme of the development spectrum; the coaches will have to judge as to the exception made and how far up or down the weight classes a boy should be allowed to wrestle.

Injuries

All injuries should be treated immediately, even the minor ones. Most injuries will be restricted to bumps and bruises, scrapes, and occasionally a sore muscle. This does not eliminate the possibility of a broken bone or some type of dislocation. It is therefore important that medical help can be easily obtained. The mats and all equipment should be kept clean and frequently disinfected to guard against the possible spread of infections.

PROGRAM GUIDELINES

The following guidelines are for use as specific standards to be followed in setting up an elementary or junior high school wrestling program. They limit the instructor as to what he can or cannot use in a specific spectrum of procedures.

Period Number and Length

The number of periods per match should be no more than three. Period length should be no more than sixty seconds in the elementary and two minutes in the junior high. This could be done in one of the following ways: straight running time or total wrestling time. The first period could also be shortened to thirty seconds for elementary and one minute for junior high with the remaining two periods running for a longer period of time.

Practice Session

Practice sessions should last no longer than one hour. It must be remembered that the younger students become fatigued quickly and have short attention spans. If practices are allowed to last too long many of the students will begin to lose interest, get tired, and become more susceptible to injury. The junior high wrestler being more mature would be able to tolerate a longer practice time.

Program Length

The program should last no longer than three to four weeks for the elementary or if practice is not scheduled daily the unit could extend six weeks. The junior high could be six to eight weeks but in no case longer than the high school season. It must again be remembered that we're not building varsity wrestlers. The object of the program is to have fun and learn a little about wrestling.

Types of Programs

There are several ways in which an elementary school wrestling program can be conducted:

1. Physical education classes.
2. After school intramurals.
3. Saturday intramurals.
4. Through local organizations: YMCA, Jaycees, etc.
5. AAU

Tournaments

All tournament pairing should be arranged according to age and weight. Wrestling weight classes for all tournaments should be divided every five to seven pounds depending on the number of participants in the program. One method sometimes used is the arranging of every participant in the program in order by weight from the lightest to the heaviest. Starting with the lightest, divided into groups of four or eight until everyone has been included. If groupings of four are used then every boy would wrestle twice and you would have first, second, third, and fourth place decided.

26

Coach-player Ratio

No more than sixteen participants should be allowed to practice with an instructor or coach at one time. This will develop a better learning situation and provide for more direct supervision.

Mats

Wrestling mats should be provided during the wrestling program. If wrestling mats are not available, then gym mats may be used. They should be held together with some type of mat cover. At no time should boys be allowed to wrestle on any other surface.

Clothing

All students should be required to wear gym clothing and tennis shoes. If this cannot be done and street clothes must be worn, all belts, pocket articles, and sharp objects should be removed from the student before he participates in a match or practice.

Head Gear

The use of head gear is a requirement for varsity wrestlers. It is highly recommended for all age wrestlers to protect the ears from possible injury.

Showering Facilities

It is highly recommended that showering facilities be available for the students' use. When they are available, it should be a requirement that every one take a shower. However, there is always the shy person and the embarrassment that could result. It is then the coach's responsibility to see that it is kept at a minimum. In places where showers are not available or space is not adequate to accommodate a large turnout, exceptions should be made. Make sure all participants have cooled off and are properly dressed before leaving for home.

CONCLUSION

The development of a sound wrestling program takes hours of hard work. A coach must spend time planning and replanning, changing methods of approach and procedures to be followed in order to develop a good program. He must spend time at clinics and classes gathering information from outside sources, including the review of wrestling literature. Working with the students is only a part of any wrestling program.

We believe that the recommendations and guidelines found in this chapter will aid the coach in the development and justification of his wrestling program for elementary and junior high school wrestlers. There is room for change in all the items discussed. This is a must, for all situations are different depending upon what circumstances the program was built. The important thing is that a program framework has been developed.

3

Wrestling Activities and Moves

The wrestling activities that comprise the main body of techniques found in an elementary and junior high school wrestling program should be covered during actual wrestling instruction. These activities are broken down into five main categories: warm-up activities, wrestling drills, lead-up games, combative activities, and wrestling moves. The activities included in this book are those selected as acceptable for use with a beginning wrestling program.

WARM-UP ACTIVITIES

The following warm-up activities should precede the actual wrestling done during a practice session. The extent of their use is left to the discretion of the instructor or coach but should include bending, stretching, and flexing such as would be experienced during the actual wrestling activities. The jumping jacks, trunk twisters, toe touchers, push-ups, sit-ups, hurdling exercises, forward roll, backward roll, neck bridging, and running in place are activities acceptable for use in a beginning wrestling program.

29

Jumping Jacks (two counts)

From a standing position, feet together, arms at side (Figure 1-1), jump to position with arms extended above head and legs apart (Figure 1-2). Ten repetitions.

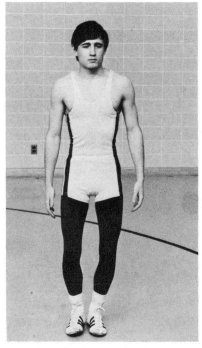

Figure 1-1.

Figure 1-2.

Trunk Twister (four counts)

From a standing position, legs apart, hands on hips (Figure 2-1), rotate trunk of body forward (Figure 2-2), right (Figure 2-3), back (Figure 2-4), left (Figure 2-5), and forward. Repeat ten times to right and ten times to left.

Figure 2-1.

Figure 2-2.

Figure 2-3.

Figure 2-4.

Figure 2-5.

Toe Touchers (four counts)

From a standing position, legs apart, arms straight out to side (Figure 3-1), touch right toe with left hand keeping arms and legs straight (Figure 3-2). Return to original position (Figure 3-3). Repeat exercise to other side (Figure 3-4). Ten repetitions.

Figure 3-1.

Figure 3-2.

Figure 3-3.

Figure 3-4.

Push-ups (two counts)

From a front leaning rest position, chest touching floor, body straight (Figure 4-1), push up as far as possible (Figure 4-2). Return to starting position. Ten repetitions.

Figure 4-1.

Figure 4-2.

Bent Leg Sit-ups (two counts)

Lying on back, knees bent, hands behind head (Figure 5-1), sit up so elbows are touching knees (Figure 5-2). Return to starting position (Figure 5-3). Twenty repetitions.

Figure 5-1.

Figure 5-2.

Figure 5-3.

34

Hurdling Exercise

Sitting on floor, one leg straight out in front, the other leg tucked back (Figure 6-1), lean forward touching hands to toe of extended leg (Figure 6-2). Also touch chin to knee. Next, lean back so back touches floor (Figure 6-3). Complete 20 seconds of stretching with each leg forward.

Figure 6-1.

Figure 6-2.

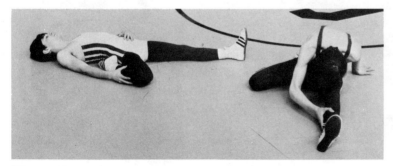

Figure 6-3.

Forward Roll

Start from a crouched position with both hands and feet on mat (Figure 7-1). Tuck head and roll forward (Figure 7-2) to starting position (Figures 7-3 and 7-4). Complete a number of rolls without stopping.

Figure 7-2.

Figure 7-1.

Figure 7-3.

Figure 7-4.

Backward Roll

Start from a crouched position with both hands and feet on mat (Figure 8-1), push back (Figure 8-2). Place hands on mat beside head to help obtain original position (Figures 8-3 and 8-4). Complete a number of rolls without stopping.

Figure 8-1.

Figure 8-2.

ure 8-3.

Figure 8-4.

Neck Bridging

Lying on back (Figure 9-1), raise body so the two supporting points are the head and feet (Figure 9-2). Turn stomach down for a front bridge (Figure 9-3). Hold each position for five seconds.

Figure 9-1.

Figure 9-2.

Figure 9-3.

Running in Place (ten, fifteen, or twenty seconds)

Run in one spot, lifting knees as high as possible. Interchange fast and slow pace (Figure 10-1).

Figure 10-1.

WRESTLING DRILLS

The following drills are for use in the development of specific skills in wrestling. Their use will aid the instructor or coach in developing the student's speed, balance, and agility in wrestling. The stance, referee's position, hand grips, knee tap (open and closed stance), spinning, riding, sit-out, switch-over, counter drills, and hand drills are considered acceptable for an elementary or junior high school wrestling program.

Figure 11-1.

Figure 11-2.

Open Stance

Body weight should be on balls of feet with feet spread to about shoulder width. Knees should be bent slightly with back straight and head up, eyes looking at opponent's mid-section. Hands and arms should be in front ready for either a defensive or offensive maneuver. It is very important to be able to move in all directions. Figures 11-1 and 11-2 show both the front and side views of the proper open stance.

Closed or Tie-up Stance

This is the same basic position as open stance except right hand would be placed around opponent's neck. Left hand could be placed on the tricep, bicep, wrist, or elbow. Head could be placed close to opponent's or out in front. Keep eyes on opponent's mid-section. Examples of different tie-up positions are Figures 12-1 through 12-6.

Figure 12-1.

Figure 12-2.

Figure 12-3.

Figure 12-

Figure 12-5.

Figure 12-6.

Referee's Position (down)

Wrestler must be on both hands and knees with hands at least twelve inches in front of knees. Weight of body should be back with hands touching mat lightly, fingers pointing ahead. Elbows can be slightly bent. This position will allow for fast reaction of bottom man. Head should be up looking at referee (Figure 13-1). Figures 13-2 and 13-3 show two different techniques in positioning the feet.

Figure 13-1.

Figure 13-2.

Figure 13-3.

43

Referee's Position (up-man)

Wrestler can be on either side of opponent with an arm around opponent's waist, hand on navel. The other arm must be placed in a position on elbow with thumb pointed inward and fingers on the outside. Head should be centered down opponent's back with eyes of referee (Figure 13-4).

Figure 13-4.

Wrestler's Grip

The most difficult grip to break in wrestling is the one where the fingers are interlocked and the thumbs are blocking the ends (Figure 14-1). This type of grip will prevent an opponent from being able to work on the fingers in attempting to break a hold.

Figure 14-1.

Knee Tap Drill (open)

From an open stance position, try to maneuver into a position where it is possible to touch or slap lightly opponent's knee (Figure 15-1 and 15-2). Opponent will be attempting to do the same (Figure 15-3). Concentrate on keeping a good stance at all times. A wrestler should be diligent and concentrate on defense as well as offense.

Figure 15-1.

Figure 15-2.

Figure 15-3.

Knee Tap Drill (closed)

From a closed or tie-up position, attempt to touch or slap lightly opponent's knee (Figure 16-1). Opponent will again be attempting to do the same (Figures 16-2 and 16-3). Keep weight on balls of feet and protect legs.

gure 16-1.

Figure 16-2.

Figure 16-3.

Spinning Drill

Bottom man is on all fours. Top man will place his chest on opponent's back (Figure 17-1). Top man will then spin around opponent as many times as he can in a given period of time (Figure 17-2). He can use his hands for balance. He should not cross his leg as he spins (Figure 17-3). Bottom man can stick out hand to reverse direction of top man (Figure 17-4).

Figure 17-1.

Figure 17-2.

Figure 17-3.

Figure 17-4.

Riding or Floating Drill

Bottom wrestler will be down on all fours. Top man will place his chest on opponent's back (Figure 18-1). He can then place his hands on opponent's shoulders or have them locked behind his own back (Figure 18-2). Staying on all fours, bottom man will move in all directions attempting to lose opponent (Figures 18-3 and 18-4). Top man will attempt to stay with opponent as long as possible. After fifteen seconds, reverse positions.

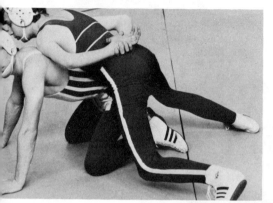

gure 18-1.

Figure 18-2.

ure 18-3.

Figure 18-4.

Sit-Out Drill

From a down referee's position (Figure 19-1), wrestler will sit through and come to rest on buttocks (Figures 19-2, 19-3). From this position, he will return to starting position (Figure 19-4, 19-5). Repeat drill continuously for ten seconds. Have each boy keep track of how many repetitions he does each ten-second period.

Figure 19-1.

Figure 19-2.

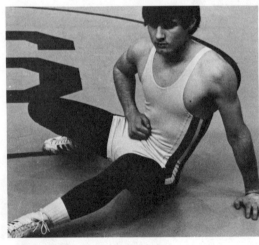

Figure 19-4.

Figure 19-3.

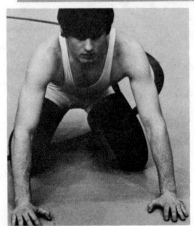

Figure 19-5.

Switch Over Drill

Wrestler will be in a front leaning rest position (Figure 20-1). On the command *go* he will reverse position so his back is toward the mat (Figures 20-2 and 20-3). Return to original position the same way he crossed over (Figures 20-4 and 20-5). Repeat drill as many times as possible in a ten-second time period.

ure 20-1.

Figure 20-2.

Figure 20-3.

Figure 20-4.

Figure 20-5.

Counter or Sprawl Drill

From an open stance (Figure 21-1), sprawl to a front leaning rest position (Figures 21-2 and 21-3). Draw to knees (Figure 21-4) and then to a standing stance position (Figures 21-5 and 21-6). Repeat drill as many times as possible in fifteen seconds.

Figure 21-2.

Figure 21-1.

Figure 21-3.

Figure 21-4.

Figure 21-5.

Figure 21-6.

Hand Slap Drill

This drill is designed mainly to develop swift reaction time. Wrestlers start one with palms down, the other with palms up, directly over each other (Figure 22-1). The bottom man will try and slap the top of opponent's hands before he can move hands away (Figures 22-2 and 22-3). Each wrestler will make five attempts.

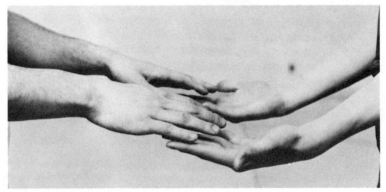

Figure 22-1.

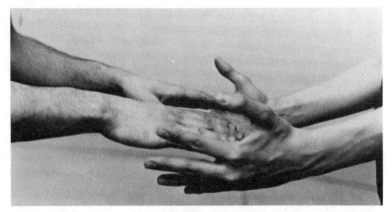

Figure 22-2.

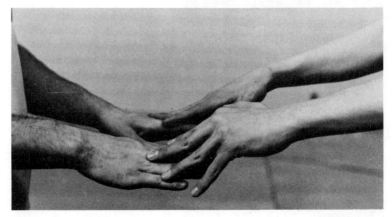

Figure 22-3.

Handzy Drill

Each wrestler will try to gain control of opponent's hands (Figures 23-1, 23-2, and 23-3). In order to prevent this from happening, a wrestler must also concentrate on defensive.

Figure 23-1.

Figure 23-3.

Figure 23-2.

LEAD-UP ACTIVITIES

Lead-up activities serve as a preliminary activity to an actual wrestling match. It will give an instructor or coach a chance to determine if the student has developed a knowledge of different wrestling moves. Circle takedown wrestling, king of the circle, simple chain wrestling, situation wrestling, counter takedown, quick move, and spurt wrestling are lead-up activities that could be used.

Circle Takedown Wrestling

Form a circle of six wrestlers putting a seventh in the center. Number the wrestlers on the outside one through six. Start by calling out a number. That person will then attempt to take the center person down. If he is successful, he will take the center position. The defeated wrestler will take his successor's former number and position. A new number will then be called out. An individual should not stay in the center more than four times (Figure 24-1).

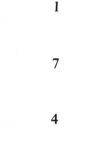

Figure 24-1.

King of the Circle

A group of fifteen or more wrestlers are standing within a circle on the wrestling mat. The number will vary depending on the size of the circle. On the command *go* they will try to push or pull everyone else out of the circle. Once a wrestler has been forced out, he cannot go back in until the next round. The last one in is the king of the circle (Figure 24-2).

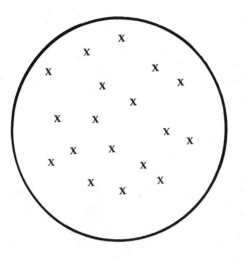

Figure 24-2.

Simple Chain Wrestling

The object of this activity is to go through a series of maneuvers in a row without stopping. The wrestlers should work for correct technique and speed of execution. The coach should have all the chains planned out ahead of time. An example of a chain could be: sit out, sit out, side roll to pin (half nelson). The other wrestler would just follow and act as a set-up.

Situation Wrestling

Put the wrestlers in different situations that might arise during a match. Have them start wrestling from that position. Examples of situations could be: sit out position (Figure 25-1), pinning combination (Figure 25-2), over and under ride (Figure 25-3), single leg ride (Figure 25-4), standing position two on one (Figure 25-5). The coach should also have these planned out in advance.

Figure 25-1.

Figure 25-2.

Figure 25-3.

Figure 25-4.

Figure 25-5.

Counter Takedown Activity (or drill)

Start with two wrestlers in an open stance position, one with hands locked behind back and the other in a set position. Man in set position can attempt any takedown he wishes from any position. His opponent *cannot* react until contact has been made by first wrestler. Wrestle for a period of ten seconds (Figures 26-1, 26-2, 26-3).

Figure 26-1.

Figure 26-2.

Figure 26-3.

Quick Move Activity (or drill)

The object of this activity is to complete as many moves as possible in a given period of time. Time periods can last from ten to fifteen seconds. The same maneuver can be used or a number of different maneuvers can be used. Examples: double leg take down, sit outs, etc.

Spurt Wrestling

Two wrestlers will wrestle for ten seconds trying to gain advantage or improve the position they already have. This activity can be used very effectively from a referee's position in developing quick reactions upon the command *Ready Wrestle.*

COMBATIVE ACTIVITIES

The combative activities found below are used mainly for fun. They provide a break in the wrestling practice. Chicken or rooster fighting, hand wrestling, hop and pull, line tug-of-war, leg wrestling, hand push wrestling, body bump wrestling, and elbow wrestling are combative activities considered acceptable for an elementary and junior high school wrestling program.

Chicken Fighting

From a squatting position, each wrestler grasps the back of his own ankles (Figure 27-1). From this position he will try to bump everyone else over (Figure 27-2). The last person in the starting position is the winner.

Figure 27-1.

Figure 27-2.

Hand Wrestle

Two wrestlers will grab right hands and stand with the outside of the right foot against the outside of opponent's right foot (Figure 28-1). The object is to pull or push opponent off balance (Figure 28-2).

Figure 28-1.

Figure 28-2.

Hop and Pull

Divide ten wrestlers into two teams. Each team will face the other about fifteen feet apart (Figure 29-1). Two wrestlers will advance, grasp right hand of opponent, and lift his own left foot (Figure 29-2). Each will then attempt to pull opponent to his own team. If a wrestler's left foot should touch the floor, that person loses.

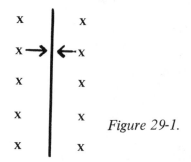

Figure 29-1.

Figure 29-2.

Hop Wrestling (line tug-of-war)

Two wrestlers stand on opposite sides of a line, each on one foot. They will grab hands and attempt to pull their opponent across the line (Figure 30-1). If one of the wrestlers should touch his foot to the mat, he is the loser.

Figure 30-1.

Leg Wrestling

Two wrestlers will lie on their backs, side by side, inside arms hooked together. Heads should be pointed in opposite directions (Figure 31-1). On a count of three, they will hook their inside legs and attempt to turn opponent over (Figures 31-2, 31-3, 31-4).

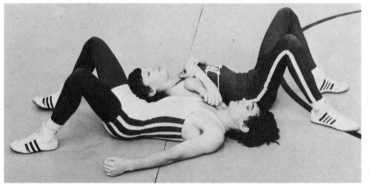

Figure 31-1.

Figure 31-2.

Figure 31-3.

Figure 31-4.

Hand Push Wrestling

Two wrestlers stand two feet apart, feet together, facing each other (Figure 32-1). Each will try to knock the other off balance by pushing on each other's hands (Figures 32-2, 32-3). The person holding his balance the longest is the winner.

Figure 32-1.

Figure 32-2.

Figure 32-3.

Body Bump Wrestling

All wrestlers clasp their left feet and hold them off the mat (Figure 33-1). On the command "start" they will attempt to bump the other wrestlers off balance using their own shoulders as a bumper (Figure 33-2). The last person left in the starting position is the winner.

Figure 33-1.

Figure 33-2.

Elbow Wrestling

Wrestlers will take a position on stomachs with hands locked, elbows together (Figure 34-1). On the command "start" each will attempt to force the other wrestler's arm to the mat (Figure 34-2).

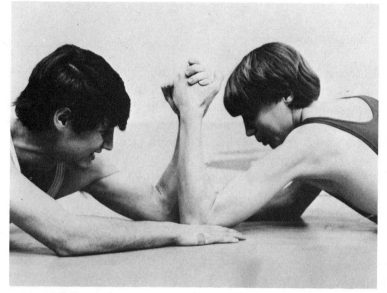

Figure 34-1.

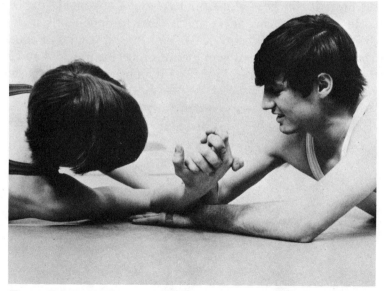

Figure 34-2.

WRESTLING MOVES

The following is an attempt to select the wrestling moves that are the safest and easiest to learn, yet possess the greatest carry-over value to all successive levels of wrestling. All the following moves are considered satisfactory for use in an elementary or junior high school wrestling program.

Takedowns

Takedowns are moves or maneuvers used by a wrestler who is trying to force his opponent down on the mat in such a manner that he ends up on top and in a controlling position. The double leg tackle, single leg tackle, arm drag, cross ankle, and elbow throw-duck under are takedowns considered acceptable for both elementary and junior high school wrestling program.

Caution—The use of takedown and stand-up wrestling should be modified. This is for the safety of the student because of the increased chance of injury when coming in contact with the mat as the result of a greater falling distance experienced during the take-down.

Double Leg Tackle

Both wrestlers are in an open stance position. Wrestler A will take hold of wrestler B's wrists with his hands (Figure 35-1). Throwing opponent's hands and arms out and back, A drops in on one knee as close as possible, his head along the left side of opponent's hip (Figure 35-2). He makes sure his knees are as close to opponent's as possible with back straight up (Figure 35-3). He lifts and rotates opponent to right, bringing him to mat as gently as possible (Figures 35-4 and 35-5). Wrestler A can initiate move by having opponent moving or pushing in towards him.

Figure 35-1.

Figure 35-2.

Figure 35-3.

Figure 35-4.

Figure 35-5.

Single Leg Tackle

Both wrestlers face each other in either an open or tie-up position (Figure 36-1). Wrestler A will step in and drop to left knee as close to wrestler B's left foot as possible, keeping head close to opponent's groin area and taking hold of opponent's left leg (Figure 36-2). Wrestler A then pivots behind and breaks opponent to mat (Figures 36-3 and 36-4). It is important to go directly to a ride (Figure 36-5). The single leg tackle can be completed on either the right or left side. Wrestler A initiates move by causing opponent to step forward or by leaving one leg exposed with weight on it.

Figure 36-1.

Figure 36-2.

Figure 36-3.

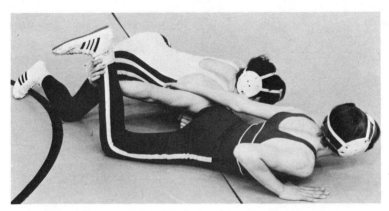

Figure 36-4.

Figure 36-5.

Arm Drag

Both wrestlers are in an open stance position (Figure 37-1). Wrestler A has wrestler B's right hand with his left hand and right tricep with his right hand (Figure 37-2). Pulling arm across body, A draws opponent's shoulder close to his, at the same time starting to pull opponent past him and down to the mat as he drops on inside hip (Figures 37-3 and 37-4). Wrestler A goes behind and gains control for riding position (Figure 37-5). He initiates move by having opponent moving forward or reaching in with right arm.

Figure 37-1.

Figure 37-2.

Figure 37-3.

Figure 37-4.

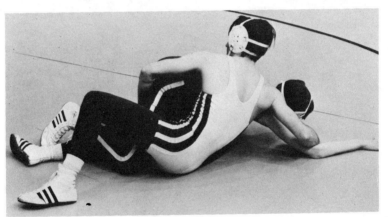

Figure 37-5.

Cross Ankle

From a closed or tie-up position (Figure 38-1), wrestler takes hold of opponent's left ankle with left hand (Figure 38-2). It is important to keep a firm hold on neck of opponent. Once ankle has been taken, he draws it off mat and forces opponent down and back with right hand at the same time he lifts left foot (Figure 38-3). Wrestler A should then go to a pinning position (Figure 38-4). He initiates move by forcing opponent to leave left leg and foot exposed or to step forward on left foot. This could be done by taking a short jab step back with left foot (Figure 38-5).

Figure 38-1.

Figure 38-2.

Figure 38-3.

Figure 38-4.

Figure 38-5.

77

Duck Under

Both wrestlers are in a closed or tie-up position (Figure 39-1). Wrestler A will take wrestler B's right arm with his right arm, throw it up and back (Figure 39-2). At the same time, he ducks under it keeping head as close to opponent's side as possible while pivoting behind (Figures 39-3 and 39-4). Once behind opponent, wrestler A breaks opponent down to mat (Figure 39-5). Wrestler A initiates move by having the opponent's weight forward or reaching with arm to be ducked under. Move can be done from an open position.

Figure 39-1.

Figure 39-2.

Figure 39-3.

Figure 39-4.

Figure 39-5.

Summary of Takedowns

All takedowns can be completed from a number of different positions in a number of variations. The ones shown here are the basic positions. The moves can be performed on either the right or left side. In any successful attempt at a takedown, it is very important to set the move up. This is why it is important to practice a move a number of times from different positions. It is important to get as close as possible to opponent on all takedown attempts. Quickness is another very important element of a successful takedown.

Rides and Breakdowns

Once an opponent has been taken down, a wrestler will use various rides and breakdowns to keep him down and keep himself on top and in control. The cross face trap and far leg, far ankle and knee, far ankle lift, near ankle and waist, near leg-far arm, tight waist, one on one, two on one, and leg ride are rides or breakdowns acceptable for use in an elementary or junior high school wrestling program.

Cross Face Trap and Far Ankle

Wrestlers are in a referee's position (Figure 40-1). Top man will reach in front, taking hold of opponent's opposite (far) arm between the elbow and shoulder. At the same time, he takes hold of opponent's outside (far) ankle on the shoe laces (Figure 40-2). He pulls on cross face arm and lifts far leg, forcing opponent to mat and over to his back for a pin (Figures 40-3, 40-4, 40-5).

Figure 40-1.

Figure 40-2.

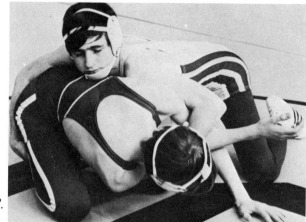

Figure 40-3.

Figure 40-4.

Figure 40-5.

Far Ankle and Knee

Wrestlers are in a referee's position (Figure 41-1). Top man will take hold of down man's far ankle with his right hand (Figure 41-2) and far knee with his left hand (Figure 41-3). He pulls far ankle and knee toward him, forcing opponent off his base with pressure of his shoulders (Figure 41-4). From this position it might be possible to go directly to a pinning hold (Figure 41-5).

Figure 41-1.

Figure 41-2.

Figure 41-3.

Figure 41-4.

Figure 41-5.

Tight Waist Far Ankle Lift

Wrestlers are in a referee's position (Figure 42-1). Top wrestler will drop right hand to opponent's right ankle taking hold of shoelaces (Figure 42-2). At the same time, he drops left hand off opponent's elbow and takes hold of waist (Figure 42-3). Lifting far ankle, he forces opponent to mat (Figure 42-4). If bottom wrestler starts walking forward on hands, top man should block inside arm (Figure 42-5).

Figure 42-1.

Figure 42-2.

Figure 42-3.

Figure 42-4.

Figure 42-5.

Near Ankle and Waist

Wrestlers are in a referee's position (Figure 43-1). Top wrestler will move behind and take hold of opponent's inside ankle with left hand (Figure 43-2). His right hand moves to "tight waist." Lifting ankle, he forces opponent to mat (Figures 43-3 and 43-4). As mentioned previously, if bottom wrestler starts walking forward on hands, top wrestler should block far arm (Figure 43-5).

Figure 43-1.

Figure 43-2.

Figure 43-3.

Figure 43-4.

Figure 43-5.

Near Leg — Far Arm

Wrestlers are in a referee's position (Figure 44-1). Top wrestler will take hold of opponent's near leg with right hand and far arm with his left hand (Figure 44-2). He pulls the near leg and far arm toward him, forcing opponent to mat with chest (Figure 44-3 and 44-4). Top wrestler should then work for a pin (Figure 44-5).

Figure 44-1.

Figure 44-2.

Figure 44-3.

Figure 44-4.

Figure 44-5.

Tight Waist — Near Arm

Wrestlers are in a referee's position (Figure 45-1). Top man will force inside arm of opponent down with his left arm (Figure 45-2). At the same time, he keeps a tight waist with right arm (Figure 45-3). He forces opponent to mat (Figure 45-4), at the same time it might be possible to come across to the other side with a pinning combination (Figures 45-5 and 45-6).

Figure 45-1.

Figure 45-2.

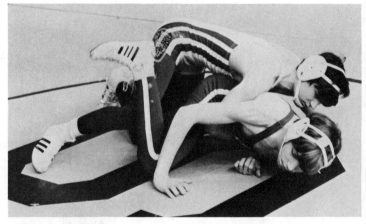

Figure 45-3.

Figure 45-4.

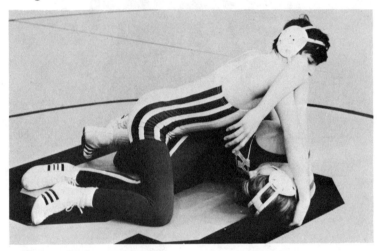

Figure 45-5.

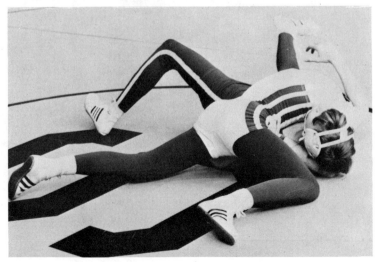

Figure 45-6.

One on One

Wrestlers are in a referee's position (Figure 46-1). Top wrestler will break bottom man down (Figures 46-2 and 46-3), take hold of opponent's right wrist with right hand and left wrist with left hand (Figure 46-4). Using his own arms as a lever, he forces opponent to mat. (Figure 46-5).

Figure 46-1.

Figure 46-2.

Figure 46-3.

Figure 46-4.

Figure 46-5.

Two on One

Wrestlers are in a referee's position (Figure 47-1). Top wrestler will take hold of either opponent's right hand or left hand with both his right and left hands (Figures 47-2 and 47-3). Using his arms as a lever, he will force opponent to mat (Figure 47-4).

Figure 47-1.

Figure 47-2.

Figure 47-3.

Figure 47-4.

Single Leg Ride

Wrestlers are in a referee's position (Figure 48-1). Top man will force opponent's left arm in to side with his left hand and at the same time "tight waist" opponent with right arm bumping him forward (Figure 48-2). He steps over opponent's inside leg and sits back on it to maintain control (Figures 48-3, 48-4, 48-5).

Figure 48-1.

Figure 48-2.

Figure 48-3.

Figure 48-4.

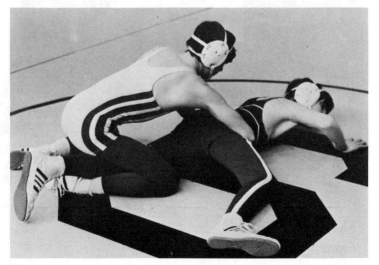

Figure 48-5.

Summary of Rides and Breakdowns

The different rides and breakdowns can be worked from both sides of the opponent. They are used to control an opponent and work into a position for a pin. It is important for a wrestler to have good balance and control with knowledge of what an opponent might do for a counter maneuver. It is important to keep body weight back and never let body parts overhang the front part of opponent's body. A wrestler should move to a forward position only when the opponent is in a flattened position on the mat.

Escapes and Reversals

Escapes and reversals are used by a wrestler trying to free himself from the control of an opponent or gain control of the opponent. The following moves are recommended for use in an elementary and junior high school wrestling program: hip roll, sit-out, stand-up, and wing-step over.

Hip Roll

Wrestlers will start from a referee's position (Figure 49-1). Bottom man will take hold of opponent's right hand or wing his right arm, holding it tightly against his body (Figure 49-2), bringing right knee to left knee, tucking into a ball shape (Figure 49-3). Holding opponent's arm tight, he rolls off hip tossing leg to complete roll (Figure 49-4). Turning left to face opponent, also maintaining control of opponent's right arm (Figure 49-5), top wrestler can go directly to pin (Figure 49-6). Wrestler initiates move when opponent has weight pushing into him.

Figure 49-1.   *Figure 49-2.*

Figure 49-3.

Figure 49-4.

Figure 49-5.

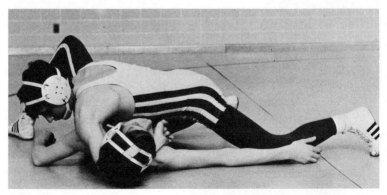

Figure 49-6.

Sit-Out

Wrestlers are in a referee's position (Figure 50-1). Bottom man will draw right knee up placing right foot to outside of right hand (Figure 50-2). Supporting weight on outside foot and right hand, bottom man will sit through, coming to rest on buttocks (Figure 50-3). It is important to have gained control of opponent's hand; this should be done at the start of the sit-out. It is important here to duck shoulder and bring right knee over and as close to chest as possible, rolling to left facing opponent (Figures 50-4, 50-5, 50-6). He initiates move by pushing back on opponent with a short bump motion.

Figure 50-1.

Figure 50-2.

Figure 50-3.

Figure 50-4.

Figure 50-5.

Figure 50-6.

Short Sit-Out

Starting in a referee's position (Figure 51-1), bottom wrestler will start a sit-out as previously described (Figures 51-2, 51-3). At this point it is important for bottom man to duck back and under opponent's arm to gain control (Figures 51-4, 51-5). Finish up by breaking opponent to mat (Figure 51-6).

Figure 51-1.

Figure 51-2.

Figure 51-3.

Figure 51-4.

Figure 51-5.

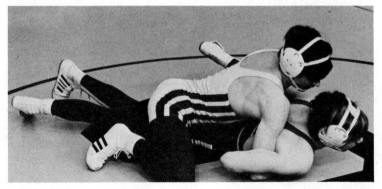

Figure 51-6.

103

Stand Up

Wrestlers start from a referee's position (Figure 52-1). This move can be initiated with either the right, left, or both legs as a lead step. Bottom man will bump opponent to set up maneuver. If outside foot should lead, he steps on that foot coming to both feet as balance is obtained (Figures 52-2 and 52-3). With elbow blocking out arm, back straight, hand controlling hand, he starts pivoting, forcing hands down and off his own hips (Figure 52-4). When hands are controlled, he pivots to a facing position (Figure 52-5). If opponent should lock hands, work on one hand off own hip (Figure 52-6). When broken, pivot same as above (Figures 52-7, 52-8).

Figure 52-1.

Figure 52-2.

Figure 52-3.

Figure 52-4.

Figure 52-5.

Figure 52-6.

Figure 52-7.

Figure 52-8.

Wing-Step Over

Wrestlers start in a referee's position (Figure 53-1). Bottom man will wing as high as possible on an overhanging arm (Figure 53-2). He snaps opponent to mat (Figure 53-3), stepping or jumping over opponent (Figure 53-4). It might be possible to go directly to a pin (Figure 53-5). The snap down and step over should be all in one movement.

Figure 53-1.

Figure 53-2.

Figure 53-3.

Figure 53-4.

Figure 53-5.

Summary of Escapes and Reversals

Before an escape and reversal can be executed, the defensive wrestler must be in a position where his base of support will be his hands and knees, weight back. From here he will be able to move in different directions depending on the type of pressure the offensive wrestler is applying. The defensive wrestler should have legs and feet clear and in control of opponent's hands. He must then move, not allowing his opponent an opportunity to flatten him out again. There will be times when the defensive wrestler will have to make two, three, and even four moves in succession before an escape or reversal can be won. This is why it is important to be moving at all times.

Pinning Combinations

Pinning combinations are used to win a match by putting and holding an opponent's shoulders to the mat for two seconds. The half-nelson, snap back from a sit-out position, cradle, and reverse cradle are pinning combinations acceptable for elementary or junior high school wrestling.

Figure 54-1.

Figure 54-2.

Figure 54-3.

Half Nelson

Before attempting this pin, bottom man should be in a flattened position (Figure 54-1). Top man will then place hand nearest head under opponent's arm and top back of opponent's head (Figure 54-2). From here, he uses arm as a lever to turn opponent over (Figures 54-3 and 54-4). The use of the other arm can vary in aiding the turnover of opponent: it can be placed inside crotch (Figure 54-5), or holding opponent's free shoulder (Figure 54-6).

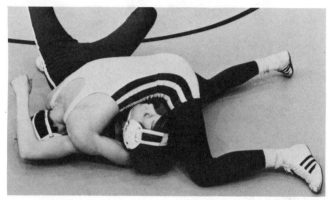

Figure 54-4.

Figure 54-5.

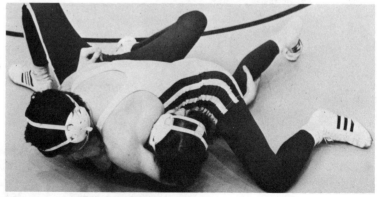

Figure 54-6.

Snap Back from Sit-Out Position

From a referee's position (Figure 55-1) the bottom man attempts a sit-out, top man will slide left hand up into opponent's arm pit (Figure 55-2). At that time, he will also hook opponent's chin with other hand (Figure 55-3). He pulls opponent back to mat and holds for a pin (Figure 55-4).

Figure 55-1.

Figure 55-2.

Figure 55-3.

Figure 55-4.

Cradle

Top wrestler will cross face opponent, taking his arm as high as possible on the arm (Figures 56-1 and 56-2). At the same time, he takes hold of opponent's opposite leg around the outside (Figure 56-3). Driving head toward leg, he takes a wrestler's grip (Figure 56-4). He turns opponent to his back (Figures 56-5 and 56-6). It may be necessary to tighten grip and secure opponent's free leg with his legs (Figure 56-7). This will aid in preventing the opponent from too much movement. The best position to initiate this move would be from a flattened out position, but could be worked from a position on the knees.

Figure 56-1.

Figure 56-2.

Figure 56-3.

Figure 56-4.

Figure 56-5.

Figure 56-6.

Figure 56-7.

113

Reverse Cradle

Top man will hook over opponent's head with left hand and put force down and inward (Figures 57-1 and 57-2). At the same time, with his other arm hooked inside leg (Figure 57-3) driving head into side, he brings hands together and clasps in a wrestler's grip (Figure 57-4). Once hands have been clasped, he turns opponent to back (Figures 57-5 and 57-6). This pin can be worked when opponent is on his knees or in a flattened out position.

Figure 57-1.

Figure 57-2.

Figure 57-3.

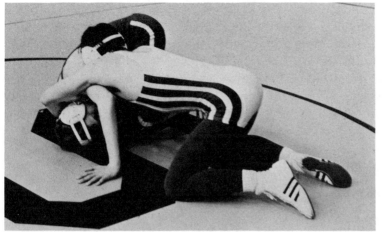

Figure 57-4.

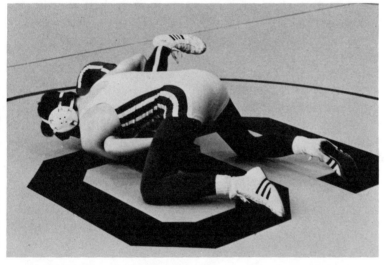

Figure 57-5.

Figure 57-6.

115

Summary of Pinning Combinations

A wrestler should be working for a pin once he has gained control of his opponent. It is important in most pinning situations to have the defensive wrestler flattened out before attempting any pin. From this position, the offensive wrestler can move weight forward in an attempt to turn opponent over. If his opponent should gain a position on the knees, it is important to flatten him out again. If a defensive wrestler can be kept in position of a pin, there will be less chance of a reversal or escape. It must also be remembered that a pin is worth six points and a decision three points.

CONCLUSION

In wrestling there are hundreds of different maneuvers with hundreds of different counters. But when you stop and look at the best wrestlers, most of them use only the basic moves. The only thing that makes them better wrestlers is their ability to execute these basic moves. This is where practice is important.

In the wrestling program it will be the coach's responsibility to make the practice sessions enjoyable yet introduce some wrestling skills. This is where the basic moves should be introduced and pressure for learning these maneuvers kept to a minimum. The end results will be a much more enjoyable learning situation and the boys will be much more willing to continue in wrestling.

4

Weight Training

The benefit of weight training for the younger athlete is often questioned by coaches. Whether it is appropriate depends on the type of training programs and the amount used. It is important to keep in mind that the goal of all sports is to contribute to the student's maximum physical development. There are many activities that contribute to the development of strength, endurance and agility. Weight training may be part of a total activity program resulting in a well-trained athlete.

At the elementary level general physical fitness activities like running, swimming, biking, soccer, gymnastics, along with strength building activities such as push-ups, pull-ups, sit-ups, rope climbing, rope jumping and ball squeezing may be used. Together these activities should suffice in bringing about adequate physical development.

At the junior high school level elements of weight training may be introduced. The young athlete is taught basic lifts through an individualized program stressing safety awareness. The following are suggested guidelines and activities that may be used in a weight training program at the junior high school level.

WEIGHT TRAINING GUIDELINES

The following guidelines will aid in constructing the safest weight training program for the young athlete. They may serve as a guide for the instructor or coach.

1. Proper supervision should always be present during weight training.
2. Students should wear a gym uniform. Athletic footwear is required.
3. Keep weight training area free of unnecessary obstacles.
4. No horse play of any type in the lifting area.
5. Know proper lifting techniques before starting a lifting program.
6. Lifting should be scheduled on alternating days with the general endurance activities.
7. Students should always warm up with some type of flexibility activities before starting to lift.
8. It is important to previously outline the program you would like the students to follow. This may be done through charting and also provides individual student records. Sample chart on page 119.
9. A one-hour period should be the maximum amount of time spent working on weight training.
10. Spotters should be used during lifting to prevent accidents.
11. Good lifting posture should be used at all times.
12. Use full range of motion in all exercises.
13. Each exercise should be followed by a short rest period of one or two minutes.
14. Two or three sets of activities should be used, students should complete all the exercises in one set before starting the second.
15. Alternate upper body exercises with lower body exercises.
16. Students should not hold their breath while lifting. Use proper breathing techniques.
17. *Do not* encourage students to overlift.

Name: _____
Sport: _____

Starting Date: _____
Body Weight: _____
Body Height: _____

	Week No: 1			2			3			4			5			6		
Date:																		
Bench Press																		
Squats (½)																		
Bicep Curls																		
Toe Raises																		
Up-right Rowing																		
Military Press																		
Pull-ups																		
Rope Jumping (timed)																		
Wall Walk																		
Sit-Ups (bent leg)																		
Push-ups																		
Circle sets completed	123	123		123	123		123	123		123	123		123	123		123	123	123

Finish Date: _____
Body Weight: _____
Body Height: _____

Key: _____ weight used
       _____ repetition/set

(Chart No. 1)

119

SUGGESTED ACTIVITIES FOR WEIGHT TRAINING

Bench Press

From a reclining position with weight level to chest (Figure 58-1) raise weight so arms are fully extended (Figure 58-2). Return to original position and repeat.

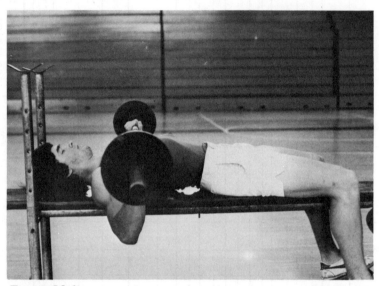

Figure 58-1.

Figure 58-2.

Half Leg Squats

Begin in a standing position, weight resting on shoulders (Figure 59-1), bend knees to a half squat position (Figure 59-2). Return to original position and repeat.

Figure 59-1.

Figure 59-2.

Bicep Curl

Standing position, arms extended with palms up holding weight (Figure 60-1). Lift weight up to chest (Figure 60-3). Return to original position and repeat.

Figure 60-1.

Figure 60-2.

Figure 60-3.

Toe Raisers

Standing position weight resting on the shoulders, front part of feet slightly raised (Figure 61-1). Raise body to full extension of feet (Figure 61-2). Repeat.

Figure 61-1.

Figure 61-2.

Rowing (Upright Position)

Begin in a standing position holding weight in a rest position, palms toward back (Figure 62-1). Pull weight up to chin level (Figure 62-2). Repeat.

Figure 62-1.

Figure 62-2.

Military Press

Standing position weight at chest level (Figure 63-1), push weight overhead to a full extension of the arms position (Figure 63-2). Repeat.

Figure 63-1.

Figure 63-2.

Pull-ups

Beginning in a suspended position grasping bar, palms forward (Figure 64-1), pull body upward until chin is above bar (Figure 64-2). Repeat.

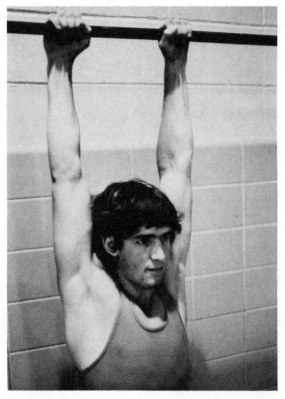

Figure 64-1.

Figure 64-2.

Jumping Rope

The exercise may be done forward or backward, on one foot or both feet (Figure 65-1, 65-2). The length of time of continuous jumping may be increased to meet the endurance needs of the individual.

Figure 65-1.

Figure 65-2.

Wall Walk

Stand with back to wall approximately two feet away, extend hands over head placing palms against the wall (Figure 66-1). Walk hands down wall until head touches mat and the back is in an arched position (Figure 66-2). Walk back up wall to starting position and repeat.

Figure 66-1.

Figure 66-2.

Ball Squeezing

The squeezing of a tennis or similar ball will aid in the development of strength in the hands and wrists.

Figure 67-1.

Rope Climbing

This can be a most beneficial activity in strengthening the arms, shoulders, and upper torso.

Figure 68-1.

CONCLUSION

In a proper weight training program it is important to remember that results are not always immediate. Each athlete will progress at his own individual rate. In many cases it may take a month or two before significant improvement will be noticed. This is especially true for the young student still going through a rapid period of growth.

5

Practice Schedule, Rules and Tournaments

This chapter contains information on daily lesson plans, point scoring, and basic rules of wrestling and tournaments that can be employed in a wrestling program. By using this material as a guide in the culmination of a wrestling program, the beginning coach will be able to develop and conduct a unit from start to finish. The more experienced coach will be able to supplement his own program and hopefully gain some new ideas. The end results of a well-planned and conducted wrestling program will be to provide positive experiences and instill a feeling of accomplishment in each participant through the learning of this truly individualized sport.

DAILY SCHEDULE FOR FIFTEEN PRACTICES

It is desirable in any wrestling program to have a specific period of practice before matches take place. Because of this, it is important for a coach to develop a general plan of procedure beforehand with program objectives clearly stated. Organization is a very important item in any athletic program. This holds doubly true when working with younger children.

All activities should be introduced under one of the following seven categories. Drills, lead-up, and warm-up activities will fall into one of these groups depending on what maneuvers they are supplementing.

When planning a program, coaches should keep these areas in mind:
1. Rules — points, illegal holds
2. Warm-up activities
3. Drills and lead-up activities
4. Takedowns — open position
   tie-up position
   knee position
5. Escapes and reversals — standing position
   referee's position
   flattened position
   pinning combination
6. Breakdown and rides — standing position
   referee's position
   flattened position
7. Pinning combination

It is important to devote a certain amount of time to the practice of individual moves with the remaining time for work on drills, situation wrestling, and matches. The following outline covers a daily one-hour practice period on the mat. This outline is only an example. If a shorter period is necessary, condense all areas equally. The junior high age wrestler will tolerate a longer practice session, with the additional time spent on refinement of moves and situation wrestling.

5 — 10 minutes — exercises and warm-up
   activities
10 minutes — work on drills related to
   different wrestling fundamentals
10 minutes — demonstration of new
   activities
10 — 15 minutes — pair off: drill maneuvers,
   practice against half
   resistance, allow time for
   each boy to go through each
   maneuver a number of times
10 minutes — pair off situation, also
   review maneuver from previous
   day
10 minutes — can be used for lead-up games,
   combative drills, matches

It is important to prepare a daily lesson plan and follow it as carefully as possible. The coach must be aware of the students' progress and be careful not to go too fast. If the team as a whole should fall behind, the practice scehdule can be changed.

Toward the end of the practice sessions more time can be spent on matches, situation wrestling, and lead-up activities. This is in preparation for tournaments that might conclude the program.

In order to learn a maneuver to a degree of proficiency, it is important to practice it a number of times with an opponent. It requires time to develop neuromuscular skills to the degree necessary to coordinate a maneuver properly and recognize different situations as they arise. It is just about impossible to learn a hold a few days before it will be used in a match. Only the moves practiced thoroughly should be used during competition. It is also important to remember that a wrestler will probably end up using only a few moves of all those he has been introduced to, so try to avoid covering too many different moves during the program. *Stick to the basics!*

The following is a list of fifteen daily practice sessions for a beginner's course in wrestling. It only covers general procedures. This plan is intended only as a guide and can be varied considerably without hampering its efficiency.

Daily Practice 1

a. Discuss wrestling as a sport; history, fundamentals, rules, contribution to fitness and health, use as a recreational activity.
b. Demonstrate stance on feet.
c. Demonstrate how to move about on mat.
d. Introduce double leg drop.
e. Introduce referee's position from top and underneath.
f. Introduce the sit-out escape.

Daily Practice 2

a. Review previous day.
b. Introduce far side roll.
c. Introduce hip roll.
d. Introduce half nelson.

Daily Practice 3

a. Review previous day.
b. Introduce the different breakdowns and rides.
c. Practice takedown covered first day.

Daily Practice 4

a. Review previous day.
b. Introduce the cradle.
c. Introduce the arm drag from knee position.
d. Review the side roll and introduce the near side roll step across.

Daily Practice 5

a. Review previous day.
b. Introduce stand-up.
c. Spend part of the hour showing the relationship between the moves already introduced.
d. Practice mixing up the moves that have already been covered.

Daily Practice 6

a. Review moves introduced the previous day.
b. Introduce the cross ankle.
c. Introduce the elbow throw-duck under.
d. Review the pinning combinations covered.
e. Introduce snap back from a sit-out position.

Daily Practice 7

a. Review moves introduced the previous day.
b. Go over the different rides and breakdowns.
c. Introduce the switch.
d. Review the stand-up.

Daily Practice 8

a. Review moves introduced the previous day.
b. Demonstrate various ways of setting up different moves.
c. Practice competitive wrestling under close supervision of the coach or instructor.

Daily Practice 9

a. All moves that are to be introduced during the wrestling program should have been demonstrated. The remaining practices are for review and practice.
b. Practice competitive wrestling under close supervision.

Daily Practice 10

    a. Illustrate the importance of moving at all times on feet and the top and underneath positions.
    b. Review moves already introduced.
    c. Practice mixing up the moves already covered and see if students can recall them.
    d. Practice competitive wrestling under close supervision.

Daily Practice 11

    a. Review moves covered previously.
    b. Introduce how a tournament is conducted.
    c. Practice competitive wrestling under close supervision.

Daily Practice 12

    a. Review moves covered previously.
    b. Practice mixing the escape techniques, faking one and shifting to another.
    c. Practice various methods of setting up different moves.
    d. Practice competitive wrestling under close supervision.

Daily Practice 13

    a. Review moves already covered.
    b. Show squad who will be wrestling in the various weight groups during the tournament.
    c. Practice competitive wrestling under close supervision.

Daily Practice 14

Tournament.

Daily Practice 15

Tournament.

Each day a coach should use some drills and lead-up activities. These will be used to supplement the different moves as they are introduced. To give a break in the practice sessions, different combative activities can be used. The daily practice sessions should be designed to be fun and not to develop star wrestlers. This objective will be left to the varsity teams.

POINTS SCORING IN WRESTLING[1]

Individual Matches

Takedown	2 points
Escape	1 point
Reversal	2 points
Near fall	2 or 3 points

Tournament

Fall	2 points
Default	2 points
Forfeit	2 points
Disqualification	2 points
Advancement	
Championship Bracket	2 points
Consolation Bracket	1 point
Superior Decision	1 point (by 12 or more points)
	½ point (by at least 8 and fewer then 12 points)

Dual Meet

Fall	6 points
Forfeit	6 points
Default	6 points
Disqualification	6 points
Superion Decision	5 points (by 12 or more points)
Major Decision	4 points (by 8 to 11 points)
Regular Decision	3 points (by less than 7 points)
Draw	2 points

Penalty Points

Illegal holds	1 point, no warning
Stalling	1 point, after one warning
Unnecessary roughness	1 point, no warning
Technical violation	1 point, no warning
Unsportsmanlike conduct	1 team point deducted

---

1. *National Federation Edition 1975-76 Wrestling Rulebook,* Elgin, Illinois: National Federation of State High School Associations, (1975-1976) p. 31.

WRESTLING RULES[2]

Inbounds   If supporting points of either wrestler are inbounds, wrestling continues. Near-fall points or a fall may be earned only while the shoulders of the defensive wrestler are in-bounds.

Near-Fall   A near-fall is a position in which the offensive wrestler has control of his opponent in a pinning situation with: (1) 2 points — both shoulders of the defensive wrestler held momentarily (stopped) within 4 inches of the mat or less, or when one shoulder of the defensive wrestler is touching the mat and the other shoulder is held at an angle of 45 degrees or less with the mat. (2) 3 points — both shoulders are held in the above position for 5 seconds or longer.

Starting Position   Top man. This has been liberalized so that only one knee has to be on the mat and to the outside of your opponent. The other foot can be behind him as well as the other knee.

Stalling   A stalling penalty is preceded by one warning. No time limit for the stalling penalty, it will be called immediately.

Dual meet points   Fall—6 points, decision by 12 or more points—5 points, major decision—4 points, decision —3 points, draw—2 points, forfeit or default—6 points.

Reversal   Defensive wrestler gains control on the mat or in a rear standing position.

Overtime tie criteria   Fall attempts, takedowns, reversal, escapes, then maintenance of control.

Illegal holds   Hammerlock above right angle, front headlock, headlock without arm, straight head scissors, overscissors, full nelson slams, toe holds, twisting knee, pulling less than 4 fingers. May not overlap or interlock hands if you have advantage.

2. Ibid. p.p. 6 - 31.

TOURNAMENT

Junior high programs, because of a more teamlike organization, will be conducted on a intraschool basis and wrestle-offs would be conducted at each weight. Only the best wrestlers at each weight would be allowed to wrestle in a tournament. This is where an interschool tournament would be desirable. It would allow all boys to participate in and possibly win a tournament championship.

Most elementary school wrestling programs will be concluded with a tournament. It is therefore important that no boy be excluded from participation in the tournament. This would also include any late comers. If possible, each boy should have the opportunity to wrestle a number of times. The following should aid the coach in setting up and conducting a wrestling tournament.

Time and Place of Tournament

The best place to conduct a wrestling tournament would be either in the school gymnasium or a community civic center. The tournament could be conducted in the evening after supper or after school or on a Saturday morning. Have the order of matches arranged ahead of time. This will allow for a faster tournament. Try to hold the length of the tournament to under three hours.

Weight Classes

There are several methods of arranging your tournament. One very good way would be to group all boys by weight in order from the lightest to the heaviest. Once this has been done start at the lightest and divide the group into brackets of four or eight participants. If four boys are used in a weight class, more champions will be chosen. It will also give each boy the chance to wrestle twice. If eight boys are used in a weight class there will be fewer brackets to work with. The use of a round robin would work very well for a wrestling tournament. If a round robin is used, the four-boy schedule should be followed. This would allow each boy to wrestle three times.

Another good method that can be used would be to set the weight classes every five or seven pounds. Boys that fall within a weight class would wrestle there. In this type, a bracket might contain several boys or just a few. When designing the different weight classes for either the elementary or junior high levels, try developing as many different weight divisions as possible. The total will depend on the number of individuals taking part in the program. You will have the largest number of weight classes where you find the heaviest concentration of wrestlers. At the elementary level, this will probably be between 65 and 90 pounds. At the junior high level, from about 115 to 145 pounds. If there are a large number of wrestlers above or below the weight classes suggested below, add additional groups to satisfy the need.

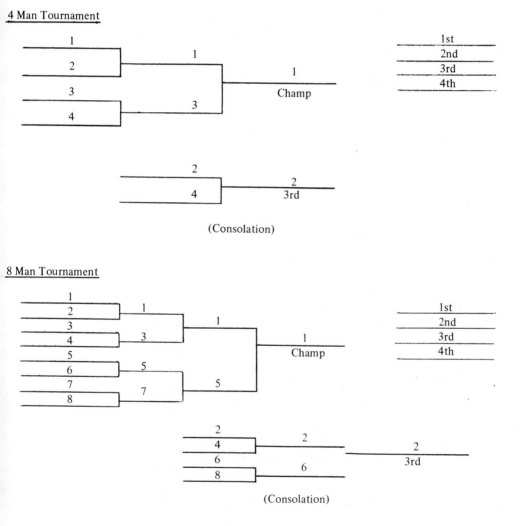

4 Man Tournament

8 Man Tournament

Suggested Weight Classes for Elementary:

- 55
56 - 60
61 - 65
66 - 70
71 - 75   Byes will be used to fill empty spots within
76 - 80   a bracket.
81 - 85
86 - 90
91 - 95
96 - 100
Hwt

Suggested Weight Classes for Junior High:

- 90
91   - 97
98   - 103
104 - 109
110 - 115
116 - 120
121 - 125   Byes will be used to fill empty spots within
126 - 130   a bracket
131 - 135
136 - 140
141 - 147
148 - 155
156 - 165
Hwt

Round Robin

Mat
| A | 2 - 1 | 4 - 2 | 4 - 1 |
| B | 3 - 4 | 1 - 3 | 2 - 3 |

Each boy will wrestle three times.

Awards and Pictures

Awards should be given to all who take part in the wrestling program and tournament. This could be either in the form of a certificate of attendance or ribbons. If money is available, both could be given. The best time to hand out any awards is at the conclusion of each final match. Have a person at the head table who will just fill in and hand out awards.

If pictures are to be taken, they should be of all boys taking part in the tournament or in an individual weight class. They should not be taken of individual winners. It must be remembered that the students are participating to have fun. It is desirable that all boys will want to participate in wrestling again.

Tournament Organization

Make sure that enough help has been recruited to conduct the tournament efficiently. You will need persons to be timers, match makers, referees, recorders, an announcer, trainer, runners, and supervisors. The best place to obtain most of this help is from the varsity wrestling team. Parents and teachers could also be employed. Have a meeting beforehand to make sure everyone knows what he is supposed to do.

The following floor plan is suggested in preparation for the wrestling tournament:

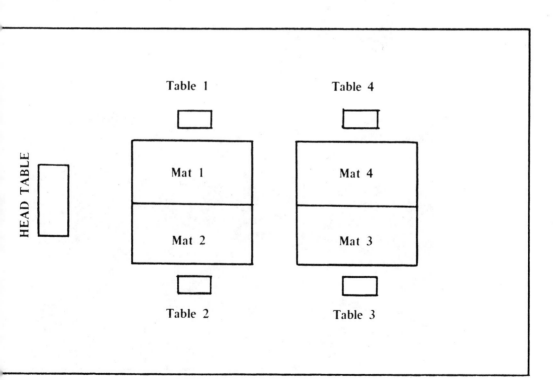

Every mat must have a referee, timer, recorder, and runner. Each person should be informed as to what his job involves. At the completion of each match, have the set of contestants report to their mat table. The results will then be recorded and runners will take the results to the head table. Awards can be given from the mat table if it is a final match of the tournament.

Before the start of the tournament, each participant should be assigned a mat. This may be done by weight class or bracket. Have all participants sit in a specific area close to the mat they will be wrestling on. Make sure each area has a supervisor. Organization will keep the tournament running smoothly.

Mass warm-up preceding tournament action.

Three mat arrangement with 12 stations (4 on each mat) for large tournament.

Letters to Parents — Elementary

It is a good idea to send two letters home to the parents concerning the wrestling program and tournament. The first would be sent two weeks before the start of the program. This would be in the form of a permission slip and introduction to the program. Include in this letter basic goals and objectives, type of gym dress required, and who is sponsoring and directing the program. Also include telephone numbers of persons in charge in case questions arise that need to be answered.

The second letter will introduce the tournament. In this letter state where, when, and at what time the tournament will take place. Also include information on the type of gym clothing each boy should wear. Invite all parents to attend. Good public relations at this stage will ensure the betterment of the program in the future.

Letter to Parents — Junior High

It would serve as good public relations if the junior high coach also would communicate with parents. This could be done in the form of three letters sent home throughout the season. There should be one at the beginning introducing himself and the program. Midway through the season a second letter informing parents as to the progress the team or individuals on the team are making. The last letter would come at the conclusion of the season with a yearly summary for both the team and each individual taking part in the program. It would be appropriate at this time to thank both the parent and athlete for participating in the program.

Tournament Action.

CONCLUSION

As the result of gathering information in this area and talking to many coaches in the sport of wrestling, it appears that the elementary and junior high school could benefit greatly from the development of a sound modified wrestling program.

Individuals at this age find great pleasure in competition with others of their own size and age. They like to test their strengths and skills in a combative type activity. If we can develop this and still give all the chance to compete and full opportunity to develop to their best abilities, then we have accomplished our prime goal in the beginning wrestling program.

Bibliography

American Association for Health, Physical Education and Recreation. *Desireable Athletic Competition for Children of Elementary School Age.* Washington D.C.: UES Publication-Sales, 1968.

American Association for Health, Physical Education and Recreation. *Desirable Athletic Competition for Children.* Washington D.C.: AAHPER, 1962.

Brown, Robert L.. *Complete Book of High School Wrestling.* New Jersey: Prentice-Hall, Inc., 1962.

Bucher, Charles A. *Physical Education for Life.* New York: McGraw Book Company, 1969.

Department of Education. *A Guide for Instruction in Physical Education.* Curriculum Bulletin No. 29, State of Minnesota, 1968.

Hopke, Stephen L. *The Selection of Wrestling Activities, Recommendations and Guidelines for an Elementary School Wrestling Program.* Bemidji State College, unpublished master's thesis, 1969.

Kapral, Frank S. *Coach's Illustrated Guide to Championship Wrestling.* New Jersey: Prentice-Hall Inc., 1967.

Loken, Newton C., and Willoughby, Robert. *Complete Book of Gymnastics.* New Jersey: Prentice-Hall Inc., 1967.

National Dairy Council. *Dairy Council Digest,* vol. 46, no. 2 (March-April 1975).

National Federation of State High School Associations *National Federation Edition 1975-76 Wrestling Rulebook,* Elgin, Illinois: National Federation Publications, 1975-76.

Reichert, John L. M.D., "Competitive Athletics for PreTeen-age Children," *Journal of the American Medical Association,* Vol. 166, No. 14, Chicago AMA (April 5, 1958).

Steinhaus, Arthur H. *How to Keep Fit and Like It.* Chicago: Darnell Corp., 1966.

Vannier, Mary Helen, and Foster, Mildren. *Teaching Physical Education in the Elementary School.* Philadelphia: W. B. Saunders Company, 1969.

Index

149